Franklin Watts

London · New York · Toronto · Sydney

Chapter One:

What Is "AIDS"?

The disease AIDS was unknown until 1981; now it has reached epidemic proportions throughout the world. Centres like the London Lighthouse have been built to care for sufferers.

This book is about a disease called "AIDS" and the very dangerous germ that causes it.

By now everybody has heard about AIDS. But many people don't understand just what this disease is all about. Why it is so dangerous? You and your friends may have heard all kinds of frightening things about it. But what exactly do you need to be frightened *of*?

In this book we will talk about what AIDS really is. We'll see what causes it, and how it can – and can't – be passed from one person to another. We'll learn some things you really do need to worry about, as far as AIDS is concerned. But we'll also see some things you *don't* need to be afraid of, and why. Most important of all, we'll talk about some simple things you can do to make sure you never get AIDS yourself.

A Mysterious Disease

Early in the year l98l a very sick young man came to a large hospital in Los Angeles, California. His illness was very strange. His throat and windpipe were infected so badly he could hardly breathe or swallow. But this was no ordinary "strep throat". His infection was caused by a tiny yeast plant called **Candida** (pronounced "CAN-did-ah"). His doctors knew that this kind of throat infection, in a mild form, sometimes happened in young babies. But it hardly ever occurred in healthy adults. Then, when the doctors did lab tests on this young man, they found something very mysterious. One very special kind of white blood cell was almost completely missing from this young man's bloodstream. It was the kind of cell that normally protects grown men and women from such yeast infections.

But why was it missing? His doctors were baffled. They thought maybe the young man had a rare kind of blood cancer or leukaemia. After a few weeks of treatment, he seemed to get better, and went home. But just a few days later he was back again. This time he had a bad lung infection known as **pneumonia**.

This was not the same as the earlier yeast infection. It was caused by a completely different germ called **Pneumocystis carinii** (pronounced "noo-mo-sis-tis ka-RIN-ee-eye"). This germ seldom attacked healthy adults. But it could cause a very deadly form of pneumonia in a person who had a terribly weak **immune system** – the body's natural, built-in protection against infections.

This time, medicines didn't help the young man. He just got sicker and sicker and finally died. His doctors were left with an unanswered question: Why had this previously healthy young man suddenly come down with these two strange infections? It seemed as if his body's natural immune protective system had suddenly stopped working. But *why*?

The Mystery Deepens

A short time later another man was admitted to the same hospital. His symptoms were different from the first man's, but equally mysterious. Like the first patient, he was in his early thirties. And like the first, he was homosexual. Both had frequently had sex with other homosexual men. But nothing else was quite the same. This young man had been sick at home for months before coming to the hospital. He had had high fevers every day. Every night he had had spells of heavy sweating. He had lost 13.61 kg (over 30 lbs) in just a few weeks. He didn't have any yeast infection. But his doctors found strangely swollen glands in his neck and under his arms. Then the doctors tested his immune protective system. They found that he, too, was missing the special white blood cells the body depends on for protection against many kinds of infection. It was

A white blood cell from a patient with leukaemia.

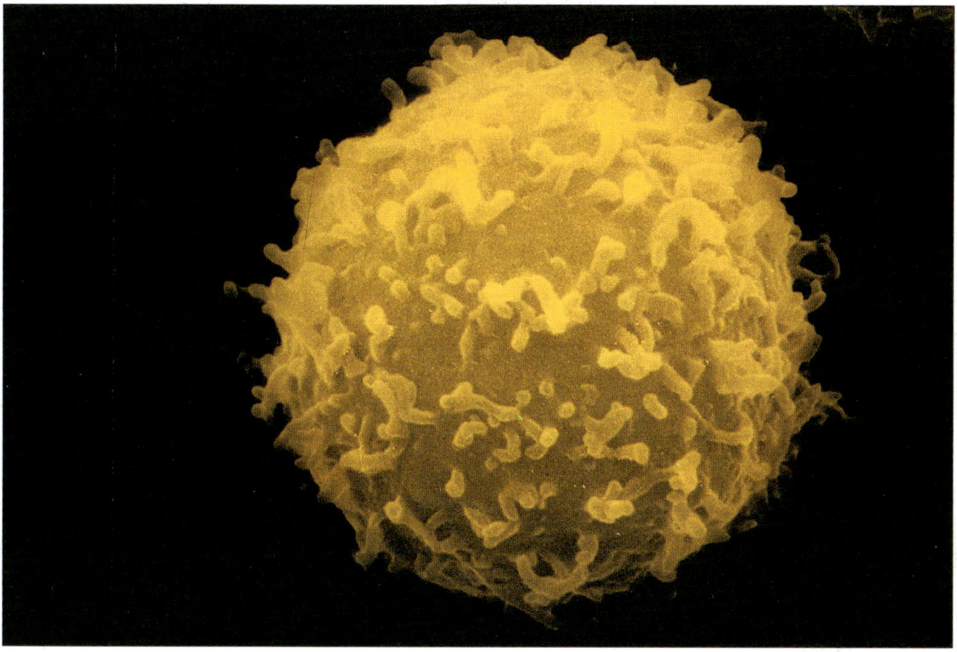

another case of a formerly healthy person whose immune system seemed to have stopped working right!

Within a matter of days still a third young man came to the same hospital. He had a very bad case of *Pneumocystis carinii* pneumonia. Like the other two men, this man was also homosexual. In addition, he had used illegal **intravenous drugs**. (These are drugs a person injects into a vein with a needle.) He had often borrowed dirty injection needles from other drug users and used them himself. His doctors did tests for those same special immune-protection white blood cells, sometimes called **T4-cells**, that were missing in the other cases. They were missing here, too. This young man was already very sick when he first came to the hospital, and his pneumonia didn't get better with treatment. He died a few days after he was admitted.

A Deadly Epidemic

The doctors couldn't believe that these three young men had suddenly come down with three completely different mysterious diseases. Their sicknesses had to be connected in some way. True, the patients didn't know each other. They had never had direct contact with each other. But all three were homosexual. All three had been having frequent sex with large numbers of other homosexual men for months and months before they got sick. And all three had sure signs that something was badly wrong with their immune protective systems. Because of this, their bodies could not fight off infections, like *Pneumocystis carinii* pneumonia, or severe *Candida* yeast infections: illnesses that seldom happen in healthy, normal adult people.

Doctors called these infections **opportunistic infections**. This meant that they only happened when a person's "sick" immune system gave them a special chance or opportunity to attack.

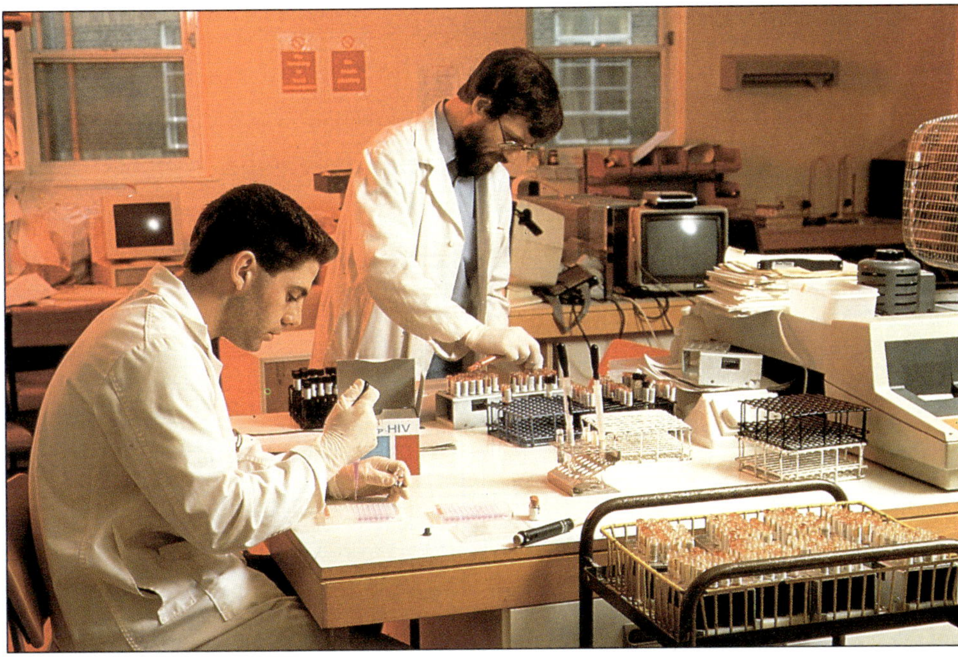

Scientists test blood for HIV antibodies.

Unfortunately, those three patients were not the only such cases to turn up. As 1981 wore on, more and more people came down with this mysterious illness in the Los Angeles area. Soon a number of cases were reported among homosexual men in San Francisco. Cases began appearing in New York City and Newark, New Jersey, as well. Within months they were also being discovered in cities like Miami, Seattle, St. Louis, Washington, D.C., and Houston. Several of these new cases were different from the others in a frightening way. Instead of having yeast infections or pneumonia, some of these sick ones came down with a strange kind of cancer of the skin known as **Kaposi's sarcoma**. This cancer had previously been very rare. It usually occurred only in elderly men. But now it was appearing in dozens of young adults! And some of the young patients with this fast-moving cancer also came down with opportunistic infections as well.

The Connecting Links

As more and more cases of this mysterious illness appeared, doctors searched hard for a connecting link between them. There were many kinds of symptoms – fevers, weight loss, strange infections, cancers. Some patients had one kind of symptom, some another. Some had two or three different symptoms all at once. True, a large number of those early victims were male homosexuals – *but not all of them were*. Some were completely **heterosexual** (people who have sex only with members of the opposite sex) but had drug habits and used intravenous drugs. Some cases occurred in women who had had sex with intravenous drug users but had never themselves actually used drugs. Worst of all, the disease began appearing in newborn babies, even when their mothers seemed perfectly healthy. Other cases appeared in certain school-age children who had had to have frequent blood transfusions because of other illnesses.

For all this mystery, there were a few links between cases. In every case, the sick patient's immune protective system seemed to have been badly damaged or destroyed by *something*. What was more, every one of these sick people (except for the newborn babies) had had frequent, very close contact with other people's bodies. In some, the contact was by having sex. In others, there was contact with other people's blood by sharing dirty drug needles or by having blood transfusions.

There was one other very unhappy connecting link between all these patients. Once symptoms of the illness appeared, *none of these people ever got well*. Some only lived for a few weeks, some for a couple of years. But one by one they all got sicker and sicker and finally died.

Facing these facts, the doctors treating these victims came to some conclusions. First, it was clear that *something* was damaging these people's immune system and causing an **immune system deficiency** – something that was *acquired* or brought in from outside the body. It could

Health Secretary Norman Fowler promotes the British AIDS information campaign.

be acquired by having sex with some other person, or by contact with somebody else's blood or body fluids. And it was the immune deficiency that was causing the **syndrome** (a medical word for a group of different symptoms) that made these people so terribly sick. Because of all this, doctors began calling the disease the "**A**cquired **I**mmune **D**eficiency **S**yndrome" or **AIDS**.

But what was this "something" that was causing AIDS? Everything about AIDS suggested that the germ might be a virus – one of the tiniest and strangest of all the different kinds of disease-causing germs. And so doctors began looking for a *virus* that caused AIDS.

Chapter Two:

A Totally Nasty Virus

AIDS claimed more victims worldwide, and the NAMES project quilt commemorated some of them. International co-operation between doctors and medical researchers led to increased understanding of the disease.

Almost as soon as the first persons with AIDS were discovered, doctors were sure that this disease must be some kind of **infection**. They thought it must be passed around from one person to another. But where do infections of any kind come from?

Over three hundred years ago a Dutch lens-grinder named Anton van Leeuwenhoek made a simple microscope. He put a tiny magnifying glass at the bottom of a small tube. When he looked through this tube at a drop of pond water, Leeuwenhoek found something surprising. He found the water drop was full of tiny living creatures far too small to be seen with the naked eye. Some of these creatures seemed to move around on their own. He called them "animalcules" or "little animals".

Today we know that some of these "animalcules" are really tiny plants. Others are tiny animals. Scientists call them all **micro-organisms**. ("Micro" means very small; an "organism" is any kind of a living creature.) Many people now just call them "germs".

Germs are found everywhere in the world. They live in our rivers, ponds, and oceans. They float in the air we breathe. They live on our skin, on the objects we touch, in our food, even inside our bodies. Most germs are harmless. Some even do good things, like turning dead leaves into soil, or helping us digest our food. But some germs that find their way into our bodies can make us sick. These particular germs are called **pathogens**, or "disease-makers".

Disease-making Germs

There are several different kinds of these disease-making germs. One group are tiny, one-celled plantlike organisms called **bacteria**. Some bacteria can cause "strep throat," a bad throat infection. Other kinds of bacteria can cause things as simple as pimples, or as bad as an infection of the spine or brain known as meningitis. Two of the most widespread sexually transmitted diseases or STDs – gonorrhoea and syphilis – are caused by bacteria. (STDs are infections passed from one person to

Viruses are so tiny an electron microscope is needed to detect them.

ONLY TOP UP
WITH LIQUID
NITROGEN WHEN
COLUMN IS UNDER
VACUUM

another during sex.) Today most infections caused by bacteria can be cured with **antibiotics**. These are special drugs that kill bacteria, or prevent them from growing in the body.

Another group of disease-causing germs are tiny one-celled animal-like organisms called **protozoans**. Malaria is one widespread infection caused by a protozoan. The germ gets into a person's blood stream through mosquito bites. A dangerous intestinal infection called **amoebic dysentery** is caused by another kind of protozoan. We're especially concerned about protozoan germs when we talk about AIDS. Two of the most dangerous opportunistic infections that AIDS victims often get – the *Pneumocystis carinii* pneumonia we've already mentioned, and a brain infection called **toxoplasmosis** ("tox-o-plaz-MO-sis") – are both caused by protozoan germs. Like infections due to bacteria, protozoan infections can usually be treated successfully with various kinds of drugs, but these infections are often very hard to get rid of completely.

As you can imagine, bacterial and protozoan infections are not very nice things to have happen to you. Once these organisms get into the body, they grow and multiply, causing harm to cells and blood vessels as they go. They may take up lodging in many different places – the throat, the brain, the lung, or other body organs. They can cause widespread damage. They may move into the blood stream and spread around that way. This is sometimes called *blood poisoning*. These germs are bad actors, all right. But another large group of micro-organisms can be even worse. These are the **viruses**.

The Virus Invaders

Viruses, the tiniest of all micro-organisms, are a completely different kind of germ. They are too small to be seen under an ordinary microscope. Scientists can only see them with special electron microscopes.

Viruses are also about the simplest form of life there is. Some scientists wonder if they are really "alive" at all. A virus is nothing more than a tiny bit of hereditary material called DNA or RNA, wrapped up in a protective envelope. Some viruses have even been purified in the form of crystals, like salt in a shaker. Viruses can't multiply or produce new viruses all by themselves, the way bacteria or other micro-organisms do. To multiply at all, a virus has to work its way inside the living cells of some other creature. It then forces that other creature's "host cells" to make more viruses, whether they like it or not.

All the viruses that we know about are **parasites**. That means they make other creatures keep them alive and take care of them. But these parasites don't do anything good in return. When they invade or infect other living cells, it isn't enough that they just make those cells produce more viruses.

The AIDS virus emerges from a T4-cell.

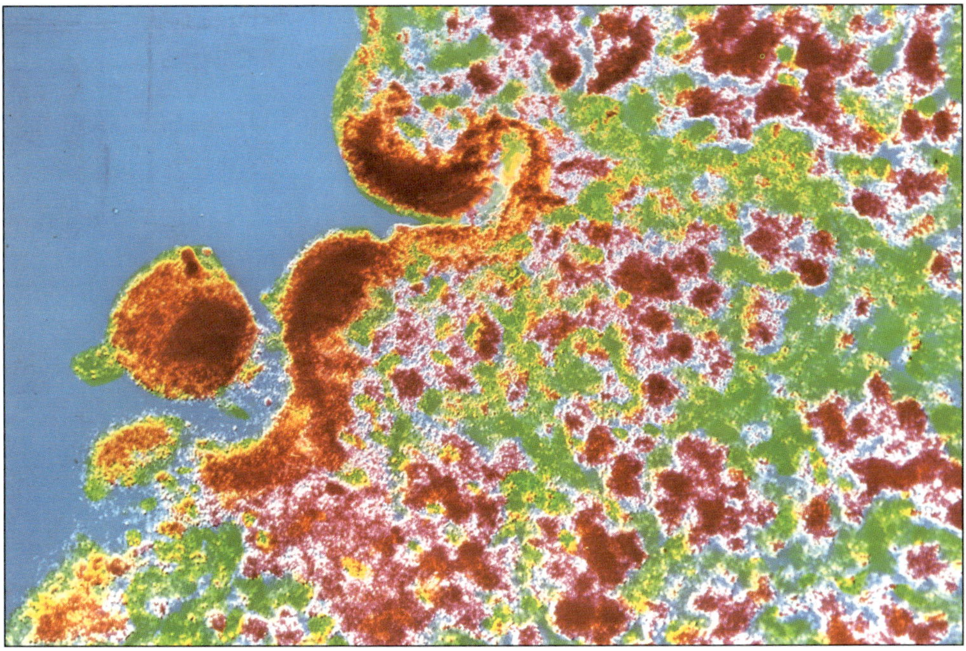

They usually kill the "host cells" at the same time. Then the newly-made viruses go on to invade and kill more cells. The more viruses that are made, the more cells get killed. When some disease-causing viruses invade a human being, they may cause a very bad infection – sometimes bad enough to kill a person.

Everybody is attacked by viruses at one time or another. Head colds, flu, measles, mumps, and chicken pox are all caused by viruses. Some viruses attack cells in the lungs and cause pneumonia. Others can destroy cells in the liver and cause a disease called hepatitis. And **genital herpes**, an infection spread by having sex with an infected person, is caused by a virus, too.

So far there are no antibiotic drugs that will kill viruses. The best we have are a few drugs which slow down the production of new viruses inside the invaded cells. But if everybody is attacked by viruses, and no antibiotics will stop them, *why don't we all die of virus infections?* Because our bodies have a special, built-in way to fight off virus infections before they can do too much damage – at least in most cases.

The Immune System to the Rescue

The body's natural immune system fights off viruses. This is a complicated army of protective cells and chemicals specially made to search out and destroy viruses and other foreign invaders that get into the body. Any time a virus invades the body, special white blood cells called **macrophages**, and others called **T4-lymphocytes** or just T4-cells, recognise that the virus is a foreign invader – something that doesn't normally belong in the body at all. These cells then trigger other white blood cells known as **B-lymphocyte**s and **plasma cells** to start making large numbers of special protein chemicals called **antibodies**. The antibodies then travel through the blood stream and clamp onto the virus particles. This makes it easier for the body to find them. Other white blood cells and chemicals can then either destroy the viruses themselves, or else destroy the cells the viruses have invaded. That way, no new virus particles can be made.

Working this way, the immune system does a fine job of fighting down most dangerous virus infections. In many cases the immune system goes one step farther. It remains alert after the battle is won. The same virus can't come back and start another infection later. We say then that the person has become *immune* to that virus. But this doesn't work with *all* viruses. The virus that causes genital herpes, for example, has a way to hide from the body's immune system. This means that people with genital herpes often have later recurrences of the infection, over and over. But for the most part, as long as your immune system is strong and healthy, it will do its best to fight down almost any virus infection.

The Search for the AIDS Germ

It's easy to see why doctors suspected that some strange new virus was causing the mysterious disease called AIDS. No bacteria or other kind of disease germ acted this way. Everything about AIDS said it was a virus infection. True, the body couldn't seem to fight it off. But that seemed to be connected to one special fact about this disease: everyone who got sick was found to have some kind of terrible damage to the immune system that should have been *protecting* them against virus infections. What if there were some new, previously unknown virus that could somehow hurt the immune system itself, so that it couldn't do its job?

That was *exactly* the kind of virus that doctors began hunting for. In 1983, they found it. The AIDS virus was discovered at almost the same time by Dr Luc Montagnier and his coworkers at the Pasteur Institute in Paris, France, and Dr Robert Gallo of the National Cancer Institute in the United States. Dr Montagnier reported his discovery first. But it was Dr Gallo

Dr Luc Montagnier and Dr Robert Gallo discovered the AIDS virus.

who proved that the newly-isolated virus was actually the cause of AIDS. Today the two doctors are given equal credit for the discovery.

The new virus was very strange in a number of ways. Most viruses contain a complete bit of hereditary material, called DNA, inside them. They just force the living cells they invade to copy it in order to make new virus particles. But this virus had only a broken piece of hereditary material called RNA inside it. It had to have the help of a special chemical called an **enzyme** to force the living cells it invaded to manufacture new virus particles.

Viruses of this sort are called RNA-viruses or **retroviruses**. Several of them were already known. Two or three other retroviruses were known to cause certain rare forms of leukaemia (blood cancer) in humans by forcing their white blood cells to grow and multiply wildly. The new AIDS virus was a close cousin to these leukaemia viruses, but it worked differently. When this virus gets into the body, it invades and *kills* white blood cells, *especially the ones that make up the immune protective system.* To describe this totally nasty virus, scientists named it the **H**uman **I**m-munodeficiency **V**irus or simply **HIV.**

Where did this dangerous virus come from? Nobody knows. Doctors now think that a few cases of AIDS occurred in America as early as l976 or even earlier. But nobody recognised the disease at that time. The first sign of spread of the infection was in l98l. AIDS had already turned up in parts of Africa, too, by then. Some scientists think that maybe the virus once infected only African green monkeys, never bothering humans at all. Then, the virus might have suddenly *mutated.* That means it changed its infectious nature in some way, so that it could infect humans.

Wherever HIV came from, it quickly spread into practically every country in the world. In the United States alone, it has caused a fast moving **epidemic**. (An epidemic is a rapidly spreading infection). In l98l, there were only a few dozen cases of AIDS reported there. By the end of April l990, there had been 132,510 cases reported in the United States, and 80,779 of those cases – almost 61 per cent – had died.* What is more, scientists believe that as many as l,500,000 people in the United States are already infected by the HIV virus and haven't become sick yet.

It's not surprising that many people haven't become alarmed and frightened by this disease. But it's very important to understand exactly **what** you need to be alarmed and frightened about – and what you **don't** need to worry about. What does the HIV virus do to the body? How is it spread – and how not? Who is most likely to catch this disease and who isn't? How can we protect ourselves against getting it? These are some of the questions we'll answer next.

** Centres for Disease Control, AIDS Weekly Surveillance Report. Atlanta, December 26, l988.*

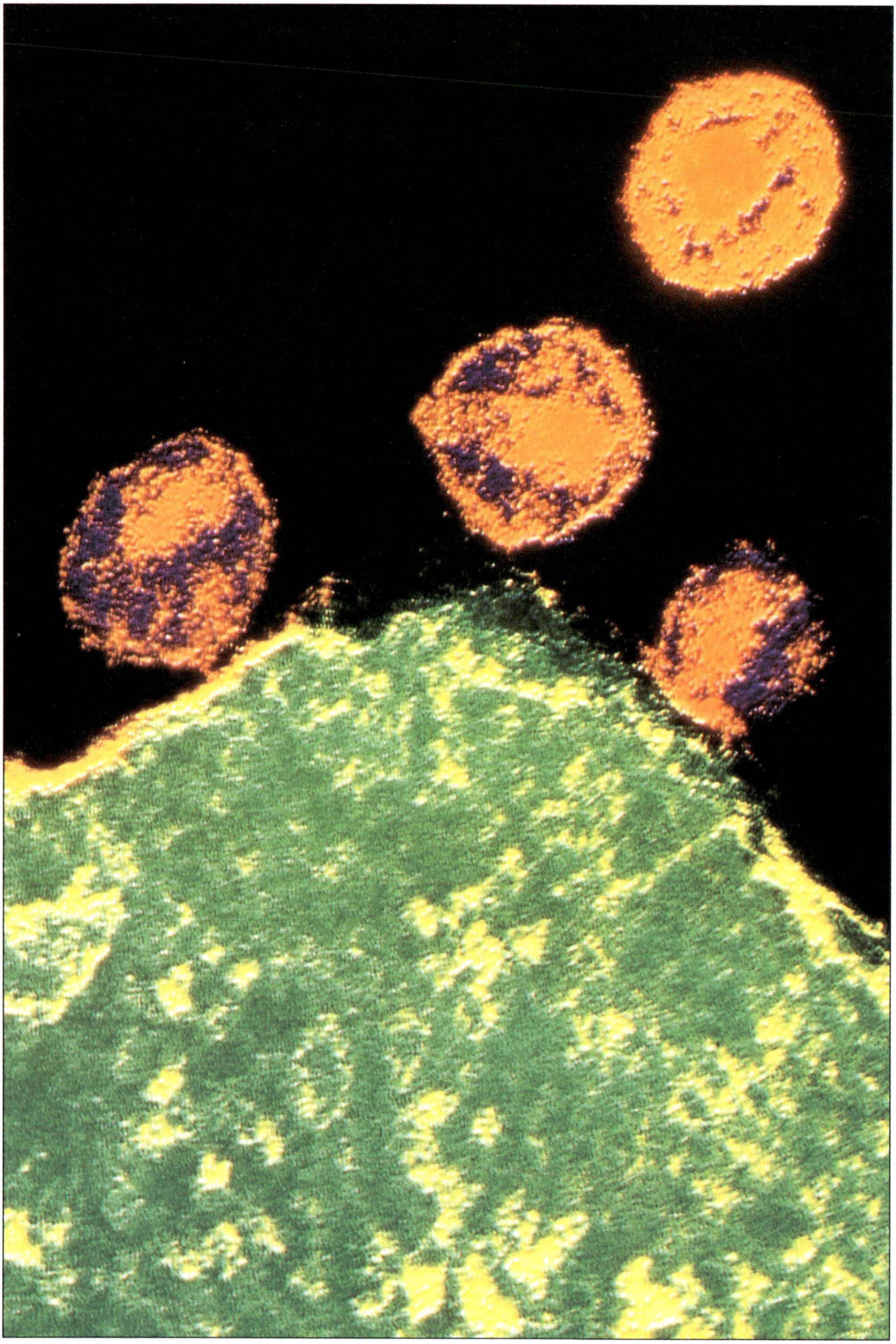

Chapter Three

A Bad Actor At Work

As research into AIDS progressed, scientists began to understand how the virus attacks the body's immune system and how the disease is spread.

Most viruses like to invade certain kinds of cells more than others. Viruses that cause head colds like to invade cells in the moist lining of the nose and throat. For this reason, they're often called **rhinoviruses**. ("Rhino" comes from a Greek word meaning "nose".) Hepatitis viruses attack liver cells. The deadly rabies virus destroys cells in the brain. And as you might guess, the disease symptoms a virus causes usually have something to do with the particular kind of cell that virus likes to invade.

Almost as soon as HIV was found to be the cause of AIDS, doctors realised that this infection was completely different from any other that human beings had ever known before. Once HIV finds its way inside the human body (we'll see later how it gets inside the body), it travels in the blood stream seeking out one particular kind of cell. This is a special white blood cell called a **T4-lymphocyte**, or just a **T4-cell** for short. When an HIV particle finds a T4-cell for its "host" (the cell that it wants to take over) it clamps onto the cell's surface. Then it forces itself inside the cell.

There the virus converts its hereditary material from RNA to DNA, which is tacked onto the T4-cell's own hereditary material. It has a special chemical called an **enzyme** to help it do that. Then the virus forces the T4-cell to manufacture many HIV particles. These newly made virus particles form "buds" on the surface of the T4-cell host. Soon they burst free into the blood stream. The poor T4-cell is killed in this process. But the new HIV particles travel on, seeking new T4-cell hosts. So as time goes on, more and more HIV particles appear in the blood stream, and more and more T4-cells begin to die.

There is one other kind of cell that HIV also seeks out as a host cell. This is another kind of white blood cell known as a **macrophage** (pronounced MAK-ro-fage, from Greek words meaning "big eater"). Macrophages are large cells. They can leave the blood stream and wiggle their way to all parts of the body. They have two main jobs to do. First, they swallow and digest foreign invaders such as bacteria and viruses wherever they find them. This means they are the body's very first line of attack against infections. More important, they team up with T4-cells to recognise foreign invaders whenever they get into the body. This helps other parts of the immune system carry on the fight against them. But when a macrophage is invaded by HIV, it is so injured that it can't do its job right. Instead of being killed by the virus, as the T4-cells are, it becomes a sort of

Actress Sophia Loren comforts a baby infected with the HIV virus.

hiding place for the virus. Even worse, the infected macrophage can carry the HIV to places like the brain that the virus can't ordinarily reach very easily. There it can begin invading and destroying brain cells too.

You might think that the body could stand the loss of a few T4-cells or macrophages without too much trouble. But these are very special, important cells. The body might be able to get along without a few liver cells, or lung cells, or even brain cells. But HIV kills or damages two kinds of cells that the body really can't do without: the T4-cells and macrophages that make up the very heart of the body's immune protective system.

In other words, this virus seeks out and destroys the very cells that the body has to count on to fight off dangerous infections of all sorts – including an HIV infection!

The Body Fights Back

Of course when HIV first finds its way into a human body, the things we've talked about don't take place all at once. Weeks, months or even years may pass before there is any sign that the virus is even in the body, much less doing any harm. At first during this time, the person is HIV-infected, but there is no way to know it. There is no test to show that the infection is there. As we will see in chapter five, it is very important to understand this, if you want to protect yourself against the infection. For some time after a person is infected with HIV, *there's no way that anybody can tell it*. It's a completely silent, hidden invasion.

During those first days or weeks, the body doesn't just take this silent invasion without a fight. After all, HIV is a virus – a dangerous foreign invader. The infected person's still-working immune system reacts just as it would to any other infection. First, travelling macrophages discover the virus particles and try to swallow and digest them. Then T4-cells, working in co-operation with macrophages, recognise that a foreign invader is present. They start sending out chemical alarm signals to other parts of the immune system. Soon other immune system cells, known as **B-cells** and **plasma cells**, start manufacturing special chemicals called **anti-bodies**. These travel in the blood stream and attach themselves to the virus particles, to make them easier to destroy.

Notice that these so-called **anti-HIV antibodies** only begin to appear in the infected person's blood stream at some time after the infection has started. The time may vary from a couple of weeks after the infection to as much as six months or more later. In some people, they don't appear for **years**. In the meantime, the infected person is walking around with the virus in his blood stream without knowing it. All that time, he or she may be infecting other people with HIV.

Why can't a doctor just take a sample of blood from a person and look for the virus right from the start? Unfortunately, it isn't that easy. For one thing, the HIV virus is far too small to see under an ordinary microscope. And it's very hard even to find traces of the virus itself in a person's blood or any other body fluid. It may be *possible*, in some cases, but the necessary tests are very difficult and expensive. What's more, they don't always find the virus even when the sample is full of it. Finally, there are only a few laboratories in the whole country that are able to do such tests. They are already busy doing them where they *have* to be done for front line research.

Once the anti-HIV antibodies start flooding the blood stream, however, it's a different matter. These antibodies can be detected quickly and cheaply by means of two different tests. One, called the ELISA test, is the cheapest and easiest to do. It is also very dependable. This makes it a good test for checking large numbers of people. Then anyone who tests "HIV positive" on the ELISA test is double-checked with a second test called the Western Blot. We know that anti-HIV antibodies couldn't be in a person's blood stream unless the HIV virus was there first. So these antibody tests are the best way to tell if a person is HIV-infected – once the antibodies finally appear in the blood stream.

HIV Infection Versus AIDS

You might think that anybody infected with HIV just automatically has AIDS. *This is not true*. In fact, there is an enormous difference between having HIV infection and having AIDS.

When anti-HIV antibodies begin turning up in a person's blood stream, we know that person has been invaded by HIV and has an HIV infection. *That is the main disease caused by HIV*. Nobody knows how to get rid of that virus once it has invaded the body. So doctors now believe that an infected person will have HIV infection for the rest of his or her life. But that person *may never* develop AIDS. AIDS is simply a late, bad-news end-result of HIV infection. It happens to some, but not necessarily all, of the people who have been HIV-infected. Since this is so very important to understand, let's see exactly how it works.

We have seen that the healthy immune system's first reaction to an invasion by HIV is to fight the virus. Antibodies are manufactured and released into the blood stream to go after the virus particles. Roving immune system cells like the macrophages try their best to swallow and digest the virus particles. In most cases this immune system reaction against an HIV invasion works very well, at least for a while. It helps slow down the virus invasion of T4-cells, so not so many new virus particles are made. About a third of the people first infected with HIV even seem to have a few mild symptoms of infection, such as fever, headaches or swollen glands, for a few days. But these symptoms, if they occur at all, quieten down and disappear very quickly. This is exactly what you'd expect if the immune system were winning the fight against the virus infection. In many people, this "successful fight" against the invading HIV seems to go on for a long time. In a few people the signs of a sick immune system may appear within a few months after infection. But in most others, two or four or even ten years may pass without any sign of getting sick. During this time, these people are **asymptomatic carriers of HIV**. That means they are thoroughly infected with the virus, and can pass it on to others, but don't have any symptoms of illness themselves.

This doesn't mean their bodies have got rid of the HIV, however. During part of this time, the virus is busy invading and destroying the T4-cells that make the whole immune system work properly. At other times it seems that the virus just goes into hiding somewhere in the body where the immune system can't get at it. It may stay hidden like that for years at a time. Then it may suddenly become active again. Some of the virus

AIDS conference delegates meet beneath banners commemorating victims of the disease.

particles that are swallowed by macrophages aren't digested or destroyed at all, but are carried to the brain. There they can slowly destroy brain cells. And there are signs that other cells in the immune system, like the B-cells that help manufacture anti-HIV antibodies, are damaged too. Soon they can't do *their* job properly, either. In short, HIV can remain in the body for *years*, steadily doing more and more damage to the immune system all the time, without any sign that it's there at all.

Enter AIDS

Sooner or later, in many HIV-infected people, this slow destruction of the immune system begins to take its toll. The total number of T4-cells in the body begins to fall. Other parts of the immune system stop working properly. As the immune system is hurt more and more, it can't do its job fighting off other foreign invaders. As a result, some alarming symptoms can begin to appear.

These symptoms can be different from one person to the next. Some people begin having daily fevers, night sweating, diarrhoea, weight loss or swollen glands in the neck or under the arms. Many become so tired they can hardly get up in the morning. Doctors say they have **AIDS-Related Complex** or **ARC** – one step down the road towards developing AIDS.

Other people have more definite symptoms of immune system destruction. Some start coming down with opportunistic infections such as *Pneumocystis carinii* pneumonia, or severe yeast infections. Others develop the cancer of blood vessels in the skin known as **Kaposi's sarcoma**. Still others have *both* opportunistic infections and Kaposi's sarcoma at the same time. And some begin to show symptoms of brain damage caused by HIV destruction of their brain cells.

These people with signs of far-reaching immune system destruction or brain damage are the ones that we say have AIDS. Today medical treatment can often help prolong the lives of people with ARC or AIDS for months or years. Medicines can make their lives more comfortable. But in the end, these are the people who will eventually die from HIV infection.

How many HIV-infected people will actually go on to develop ARC or AIDS, and how soon? Even the scientists who know the most about AIDS can't yet tell us, for sure. Doctors at the US Public Health Service's Centres for Disease Control in Atlanta now believe that most HIV-infected people will eventually go on to develop AIDS.

As for how soon any one HIV-infected person may develop AIDS, there is just no way to tell. It can happen in months but experts now think the average time from infection to symptoms may be as long as *ten years* or more. We simply don't know enough about the disease yet to make any closer estimates.

We've seen that people may be infected with this deadly virus for *years* without knowing it. They may be going around infecting other people all that time. So it's really no wonder that people are alarmed about this epidemic, and worried about getting infected themselves. Certainly these plain facts about HIV infection raise some very important questions. How is the virus spread or passed on from one person to another? Who is the most likely to catch the infection, and who isn't? What ways of living are especially risky, as far as catching HIV infection is concerned? What do you need to be afraid of, or what *not* be afraid of? Above all, *what can you do to protect yourself from HIV infection?*

To find answers to these questions, turn the page.

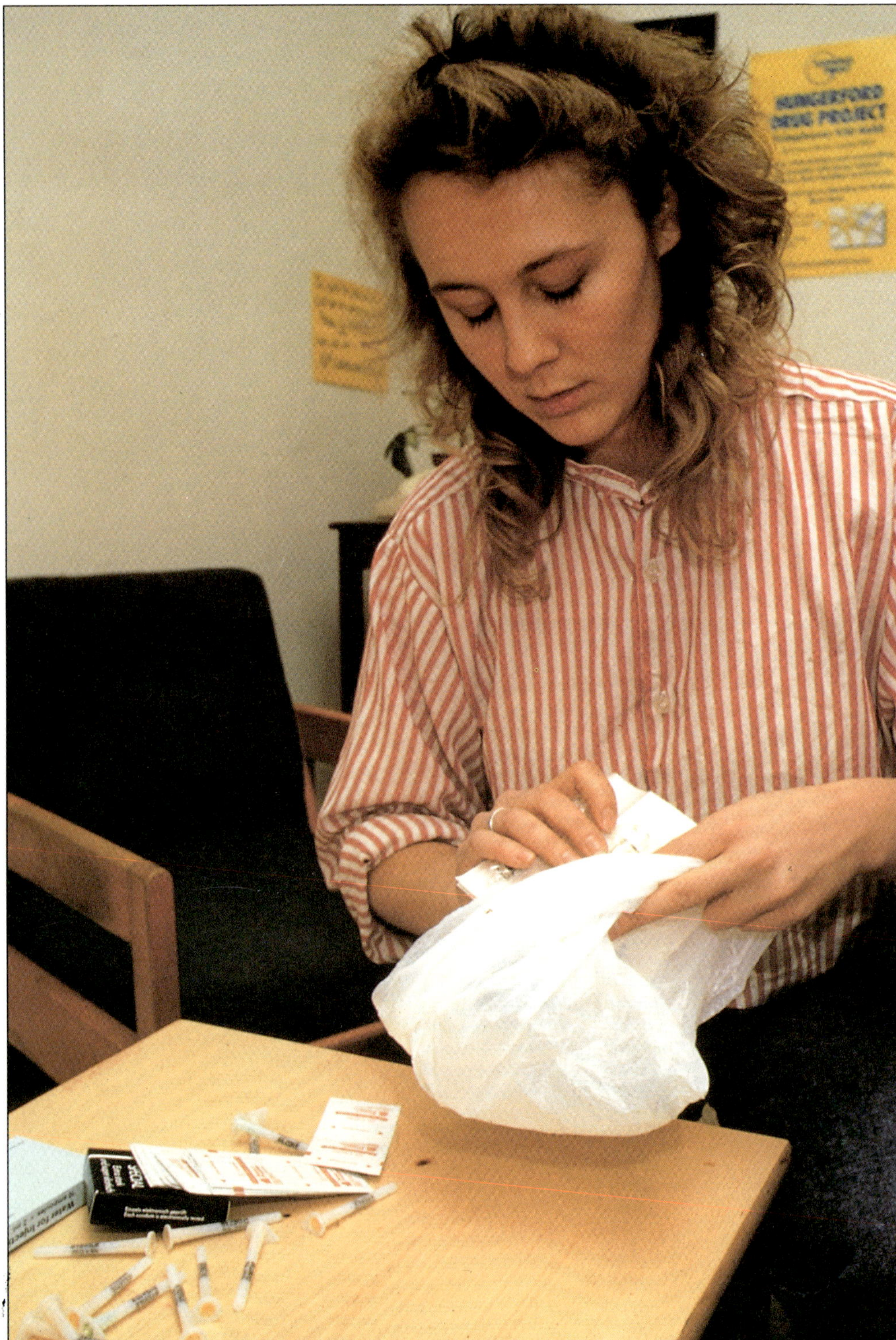
HUNGERFORD
DRUG PROJECT

Chapter Four:

How HIV Spreads

Sharing dirty needles is one important means by which the AIDS virus is spread, and programmes to distribute clean needles have been introduced in many countries.

You've heard a lot in the news about HIV infection and AIDS. It's no wonder you might be confused or frightened about the chance of catching this disease. The truth is that there isn't any mystery about it. Since the first cases of AIDS appeared in 1981, medical scientists have learned a great deal about HIV infection . Today we know *exactly* how this infection is spread from person to person – and how it *isn't* spread. We also know *exactly* which people are most likely to catch it and which people *aren't*.

The Paths of Infection

Almost every different disease germ has a favourite way of spreading from one person to another. Head cold viruses spread by way of infected droplets from the coughs and sneezes of infected persons. The virus that causes infectious mononucleosis ("infectious mono") spreads from one person to another in the saliva. This is why it is often called "the kissing disease". The malaria germ is sucked up from the blood of an infected person by a mosquito. It is then squirted into another person when the mosquito bites again. And the germ that causes gonorrhoea, a sexually transmitted disease, is passed from one partner to another during sex.

HIV is no different. It has its favourite way to spread, too. Once it has infected a person, it sets up housekeeping in the T4-cells and macrophages. Then infectious HIV particles begin appearing in great

Reaction of the body's immune system during a normal virus and AIDS virus attack.

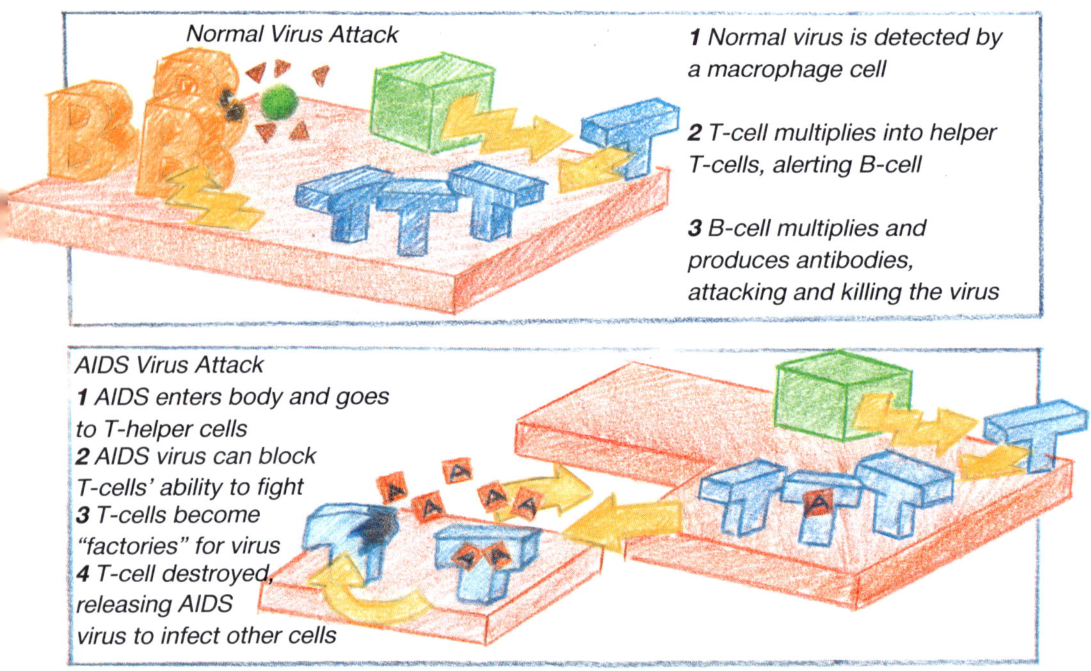

numbers in three main places in the body:

(1) In the infected person's blood.

(2) In the infected man's semen (the male sexual fluid).

(3) In the infected woman's vagina.

As it happens, these are three places in the body where lots of white blood cells – including infected T4-cells and infected macrophages – are likely to be found. So large numbers of infectious HIV particles are likely to be present there too, just waiting to infect anyone who comes in contact with them.

What does this tell us? It tells us that close contact with an infected person's blood can spread the virus from an infected person to somebody else. Contact with an infected man's semen can spread the infection. So can contact with an infected woman's vaginal moisture. And everything that AIDS experts have learned tells us that yes, indeed, *these are the main ways HIV infection is passed from one person to another*. Let's see how these routes of infection work.

(1) Sexual spread. Today we know that HIV infection is a sexually transmitted disease or STD. That simply means the virus can be passed from one person to another during sex. It doesn't matter a bit whether the sex partners are male **homosexuals** (men who have sex with men) or male **bisexuals** (men who have sex with either men or women) or **hetero-sexuals** (men who have sex only with women, or women who have sex only with men). *Anyone* who has sex with an infected person takes a chance of getting an HIV infection. This is true even if the infected person *doesn't know that he or she is infected*. The only reason so many people with AIDS today are male homosexuals (about 60 out of every 100 cases) is not because they are homosexuals, but because the infection first got started in this country among male homosexuals. Therefore, a large number of male homosexuals are already infected – and have infected their male sex partners. On the other hand, very few female homosexuals or **lesbians** (women who have sex only with women) are infected unless they have also had sex with infected men – or have been shooting up illegal intravenous (IV) drugs.

(2) The intravenous (IV) drug route. This is the second most common way that HIV is spread. This accounts for about one quarter of all cases of AIDS so far. The infection can be spread in two ways among intravenous drug users. First, those who use needles and syringes or eyedroppers to inject illegal drugs into their veins get blood into the needles and syringes. These are often dirty needles they have got from somebody else who has used them, but hasn't cleaned them. They are then passed on, still dirty, for another person to use, and so on. Suppose an HIV-infected person uses a needle and then shares it with someone else without cleaning it. That needle contains HIV-infected blood that goes right into the next person's body. This, of course, amounts to *direct contact with infected blood*. The risk of getting infected this way is *very* high. In fact, in places like New York City or Miami, this is the *most common* way HIV infection is being spread today.

IV drug users can spread HIV infection another way, too. Many of these people become infected, often without knowing it. Then they have sex with their partners and pass their infection on by that route. And sad to say, many women whose sex partners are IV drug users find out that they themselves are also infected the hardest way of all. Their babies are born with HIV infection and die of AIDS.

(3) The mother-to-child route. This is an especially sad way that HIV infection can spread. If an HIV-infected woman gets pregnant, the virus can be passed directly to her developing baby. Then the baby may be born with HIV infection. (This, of course, is a form of contact with the mother's infected blood). Or if the mother breast-feeds the baby, the virus may be passed on to the baby that way. You don't often hear much about these sad, sick babies. When they are born with HIV infection they don't live long. They usually develop the symptoms of AIDS within a year after birth, and only live a year or two longer. But we know that over l,000 such babies have already been born, with more to come, because many mothers just don't know they are HIV-infected.

(4) The blood transfusion route. A small number of people have contracted HIV infection from transfusions of HIV-infected blood from blood banks, or from special blood products made from infected blood.

Blood donors give vital supplies but before 1985 transfusions could spread AIDS.

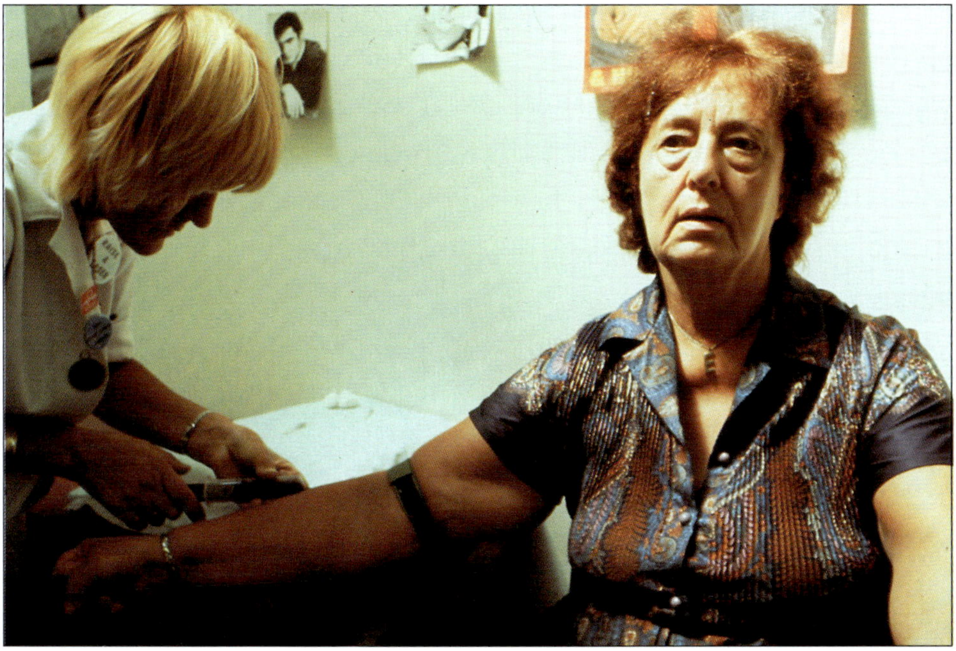

Before I985 there was no way to test donor blood to see if the donor had HIV infection. Therefore, before I985, a number of people became HIV-infected just from receiving transfusions of infected blood.

Among the worst hit were some school-age children who were so-called "bleeders" because they had an uncommon blood clotting disease called **haemophilia**. These youngsters had to have many special blood transfusions. That was the only way to keep their blood clotting properly so they wouldn't bleed to death. Several hundred of them became HIV-infected; many of them went on to develop AIDS.

These are the children you've heard about who have sometimes been forced to stay out of school. Their teachers, or the parents of other children, were afraid to have them around in the classrooms – a completely unfair, unnecessary worry, as we will see later.

Since 1985, when antibody testing became possible, HIV infection due to blood transfusions has almost stopped. *All* donated blood is now tested for HIV antibodies and thrown away if it tests positive. People at high risk of HIV infection are urged not even to try to donate blood. These safeguards aren't I00 per cent perfect. There are still a very small number of people *newly infected* with HIV who donate blood before any HIV antibodies have shown up in their blood. Even careful tests can't tell that they're infected. But new kinds of blood bank tests may soon help solve this problem.

These are the routes of infection that people really need to be concerned about. *Contacting the virus during sex with an infected person* and *contacting the virus from dirty drug-injection equipment* are real, special dangers to everyone. This is easy to understand, and it makes sense.

But what sort of things do people not need to worry about, as far as catching HIV infection is concerned?

How HIV Infection Is NOT Passed On

We know the ways HIV is commonly spread. We also know ways that it isn't spread. Naturally you need to know this, too, just for your own peace of mind.

(I) Casual contact. Many very careful scientific studies have proved that HIV infection is *not* spread by casual, everyday contact with an HIV-infected person. You can't catch it by riding in a school bus with an infected person, or sitting beside him or her in class. You can't catch it doing class projects with an infected classmate, or by using the same school toilet. You can't catch it from a toilet seat. You can't catch it just from being close to an infected person. *It just doesn't happen*. What's more, the HIV virus itself doesn't live very long outside the body. You don't

The risk of contracting AIDS is less within a long-term sexual relationship.

need to worry about catching it from doorknobs or desk tops or pencils.

(2) Coughs and sneezes. You also can't catch HIV from coughs or sneezes. The virus isn't found in respiratory droplets, or floating in the air around an infected person. This is important to know, because some viruses are passed from person to person that way. Look at the measles virus, for example. Suppose you put 100 kids who had never had measles, and had never had measles shots, into a room together. If you then brought in only one kid who had an active case of measles and just let him breathe for 20 or 30 minutes, 99 of the 100 kids would come down with measles a few days later. This is true because the measles virus is *very* contagious (that is, it's very likely to infect any unprotected person it comes in contact with) and it is carried in respiratory droplets. In contrast, out of some 80,000 cases of AIDS so far, there hasn't been a single case caused by coughs, sneezes or just plain breathing.

(3) Other body fluids. What about other body fluids – sweat, or tears, or saliva, for example? As far as sweat or tears are concerned, repeated tests have failed to find any HIV in these fluids taken from infected persons. Saliva is a slightly different matter. Doctors *have* found the virus in the saliva of a very few HIV-infected people. They haven't found very many virus particles there, and even then not very often, but they have been found there. So far no cases of HIV infection are known to have happened on account of deep or "French" kissing alone. But since the virus has been found in saliva, we have to say that it's *possible*. This means that French kissing should be avoided with anyone who might possibly be HIV-infected. There is a very small but possible risk of getting the infection that way.

Sometimes unusual situations may require special protective measures.

Some patients with AIDS vomit frequently, or suffer loose bowel movements mixed with infected blood. In one known case, a mother taking care of her very sick son became infected herself from cleaning up these infected body fluids. This means that anybody in close nursing contact with such an ill patient must take special precautions. They must wear rubber gloves, face masks, and easily washable gowns, for example, to protect themselves against infection.

4) Mosquito bites. HIV infection isn't spread by mosquito bites, either, nor by any other kind of insect bites. No one has ever found any sign that mosquitos can spread the disease.

A Rather Reluctant Virus

After seeing the ways that HIV can – and can't – be passed from person to person, there's one other rather surprising thing you should know. Compared with a lot of other viruses, *HIV really isn't very contagious*. It doesn't seem to infect people very easily, even upon close, possibly infective, contact. Of course, this is not something anyone can *count* on. There have been many, many cases in which one single sex contact with an infected person, or one single use of a dirty drug needle, has resulted in an HIV infection. But the fact is that *most* people with HIV infection have been people who have had many sex contacts with many different possibly-infected partners, or who have been sharing contaminated needles over and over again. This is important to know as we talk, in the next chapter, about how *you* can protect *yourself* from ever getting HIV infection.

AIDS
DON'T DIE OF IGNORANCE
DO YOU

Chapter Five:

Staying Free Of HIV

The AIDS epidemic is widespread today but there are ways you can protect yourself against the infection.

By now it's clear that catching an HIV infection is a very bad thing to have happen to you. Once you're infected, HIV never goes away. Nobody yet knows any way to get rid of it. From the time you first become infected, you can start passing the infection on to other people, probably for the rest of your life, even though you may not seem sick in any way. Once you are infected, there's a good chance that sooner or later, maybe months or years later, your immune protective system is going to be permanently damaged by the virus inside you. Sooner or later you may start having the symptoms of AIDS-Related Complex (ARC) or AIDS. And that can be the beginning of the end. True, there are some things that can help during this late stage of the infection. We'll talk about these in the next chapter. But at least for now, the fact remains that most people who reach this stage of the infection are going to die of AIDS.

Another thing is also true: *The spread of HIV infection is not going to go away*. This is not a "here today, gone tomorrow" sort of epidemic. The infection is already widespread. According to the Centres for Disease Control, there were a total of 82,406 cases of AIDS reported in the United States as of 26 December 1988. But that's just the tip of the iceberg. AIDS experts think as many as 1,500,000 people in the United States are already HIV-infected and perfectly capable of spreading the infection to others. And that number will go right on increasing as long as more and more people get infected.

Knowing this, it is just plain common sense to do *whatever you can* to *stay free* of HIV infection. To do this, you need to protect and defend yourself against ever catching this virus. Even if that means changing the way you live in some ways, you may need to do it in order to stay free of the infection.

Of course *nobody* likes to make changes in their lives – but sometimes there is no choice. Many young people would like to think that HIV infection is something far away from them. They'd like to think it only happens to *other* people in *other* places. But the truth is that it's not far away at all. Chances are that some people right in your own school are already HIV-infected, or soon will be. Lots of young people think, "Oh, it can't happen to *me*." But the truth is that it can. The way to be sure that it *doesn't* is to make your own decision to avoid any possible risk, as far as you are concerned. Your own common sense will tell you it just isn't worth taking any risk at all of catching HIV.

Living Defensively

The first thing you can do to stay free of HIV is to *start thinking and living defensively*. You know the facts about HIV now. If *you* were to become infected, you would be the one in trouble. And you are the one who will

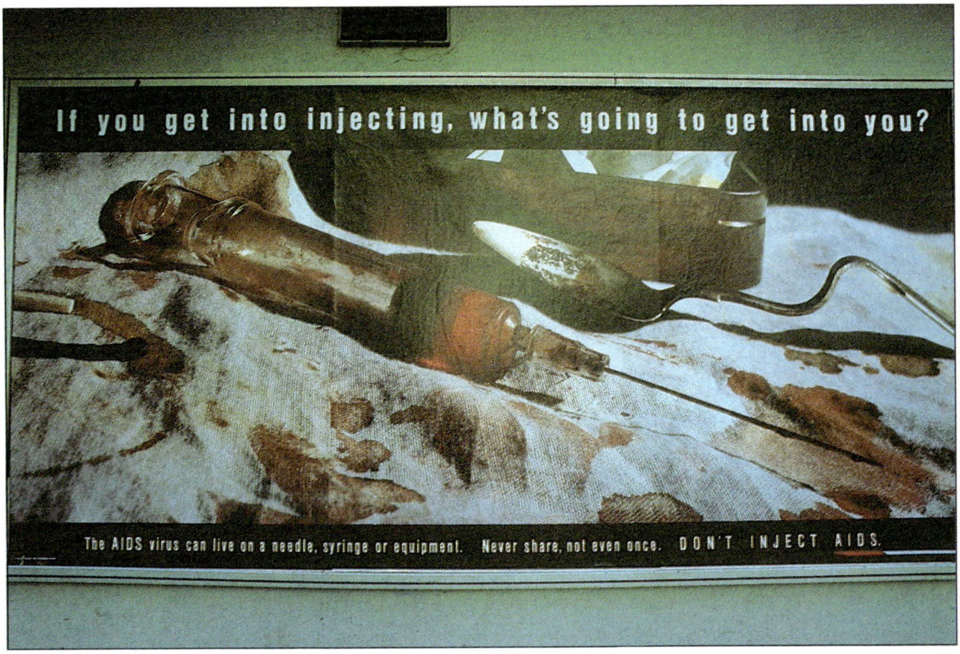

Many countries have focused on the dangers of sharing dirty needles.

gain the most by making sure this doesn't happen. "Living defensively" simply means arranging your life to protect yourself as much as possible from contracting the virus. "Living defensively" will give you the best possible protection against HIV infection. As a bonus, it can also protect you from catching other sexually transmitted diseases as well.

In order to live defensively, take your clue from what we've already seen about how HIV is spread. The two *main, most threatening*, routes of spread are by contact with dirty, infected drug injection equipment, and by having sex with an infected person. Let's see how you can guard yourself against each of these things.

Dirty Drug Apparatus

Anybody who shares needles to inject illegal IV drugs runs a very high risk of becoming HIV-infected sooner or later. We already know that's true. Sooner or later that person is going to use dirty injection equipment offered by someone who is already infected, and the infection is going to be passed on. AIDS experts know that intravenous drug abusers are already far more likely to be HIV-infected than non-users. *Nobody* in this group is safe. Right now, wherever users are injecting drugs – even in your own school – they are one of the most dangerous sources of HIV infection in the country. They are in constant danger of infection – and so are you, if you are one of them.

It's plain enough how you can protect yourself against HIV infection by this route. *If you've never used illegal IV drugs, never start – not even once, to "try it out". If you're already using drugs that way, stop just as fast as you can.* Get help if you need to, but *stop*.

Nobody *has* to start using cocaine or heroin or other street drugs by shooting up. This is something you can decide for yourself. True enough, people around you may try to push you into doing these drugs at one time or another. But if you *know* that the ones who are pushing you are truly dangerous to *you*, working against your best interests in every possible way, then you know who your enemy is and who to keep away from in order to protect yourself. What's more, nobody already using these injectable drugs has to continue unless already addicted. Even the ones who are addicted can get medical help, or help through their local Public Health Department, to overcome the addiction and get away from the risk of catching HIV infection. It isn't easy, but it is possible. Thousands of people have done it. Wherever you stand, the self-protective rule is the same: if you're not already in this high-risk group of people, *never* get into it. And if you are, get out as fast as possible.

Unfortunately, there's another way that infected IV drug users can spread the infection: by having sex with others. The user's sex partner runs a very high risk of becoming HIV-infected too, just by having sex, even if he or she doesn't use any drugs at all. According to scientific studies, about four per cent of all persons with AIDS at the present time originally caught their HIV infection from heterosexual sex contact with high-risk persons, primarily IV drug users. And many of the women infected in that way have then become pregnant and given the infection to their babies.

Obviously the way to defend yourself against HIV infection from *that* source is to avoid like the plague having sex with any IV drug user. Most of you already know perfectly well who in your scene is using IV drugs and who isn't. So it's not too hard for you to tell who to keep away from. It's a lot harder if you already have a sex relationship with a user, until you realise that *you're* the one in danger. The only answer to that is just to back away. As one girl put it, "He wouldn't drop shooting up – so I dropped him."

Sex and Your Lifestyle

The second important way you can defend yourself against HIV infection is to think very carefully about your whole attitude towards having sex, whether you already are, or whether that's still somewhere in your future. We've seen that HIV infection is a sexually transmitted disease. That's the main way a person can get infected. We also know that people who have lots and lots of sex contacts with lots of different partners are at much higher risk of catching HIV infection than people who are very, very careful and fussy about choosing just one sex partner. That shouldn't be surprising. After all, the more people you have sex with and the more often, the greater the chance that sooner or later you're going to end up having sex with an HIV-infected person. So what can *you* do about this, in order to live defensively? Actually there are several low-risk, self-defensive things you can do to protect yourself:

(l) Decide not to have sex, for the time being. This goes by fancy names such as "celibacy" or "abstinence", which just mean "no sex at all with anybody else". When we're talking about a virus infection that is spread from one person to another during sex, saying "no" or "not now" to sex is about as low-risk as you can get. Many religions – and many families – have always encouraged "no sex before marriage". The threat of HIV infection is just one more good reason to think carefully about this choice. True, for most young people, "no sex at all" is not going to work very well *forever*. But for limited periods of time, or under certain circumstances, it can make a lot of sense.

One thing is certain. If you decide not to have sex with anybody for the time being, and then *don't*, you are not going to catch HIV infection. This is probably the best kind of protection you can find. And lots of young people are deciding that casual sex with just about anybody around is not worth the risk. Later, when sex is a part of a long-lasting, loving relationship with another person, the risk will be far smaller.

(2) Many partners vs. one partner. If "no sex at all" is not a good answer for you, then what kinds of sex relationships make the most sense to defend yourself against HIV infection, and what kinds don't?

It's just common sense that having sex with only one partner and nobody else ought to be far safer than having sex with lots of different partners, any one of whom might be infected. What we know about HIV infection bears that out. In fact, a long-term, single-partner sexual relationship between two persons, without any sex outside that relationship, seems to be as free of risk of HIV infection as any sex relationship can get.

(3) Protecting yourself in a risky situation. But what can you do when you *just don't know* whether a sex partner might already be HIV-infected or not? Just go ahead and take chances? Common sense tells you that's not very smart. But there's one simple thing you *can* do to protect yourself from HIV infection in the case of *any* questionable sexual contact. You can insist and demand that a simple latex rubber condom be used during sex – whether you are a girl or a boy.

A condom (sometimes called a "rubber" or "safety") is a tube of very thin rubber that is rolled down over the boy's penis before sex. Condoms are inexpensive. You can buy them without a doctor's prescription at any chemist's shop. People have used them for years to prevent unwanted pregnancies and to protect themselves against many sexually transmitted diseases. Used during sex, a condom will protect *both* partners against

Many types of condom are now available.

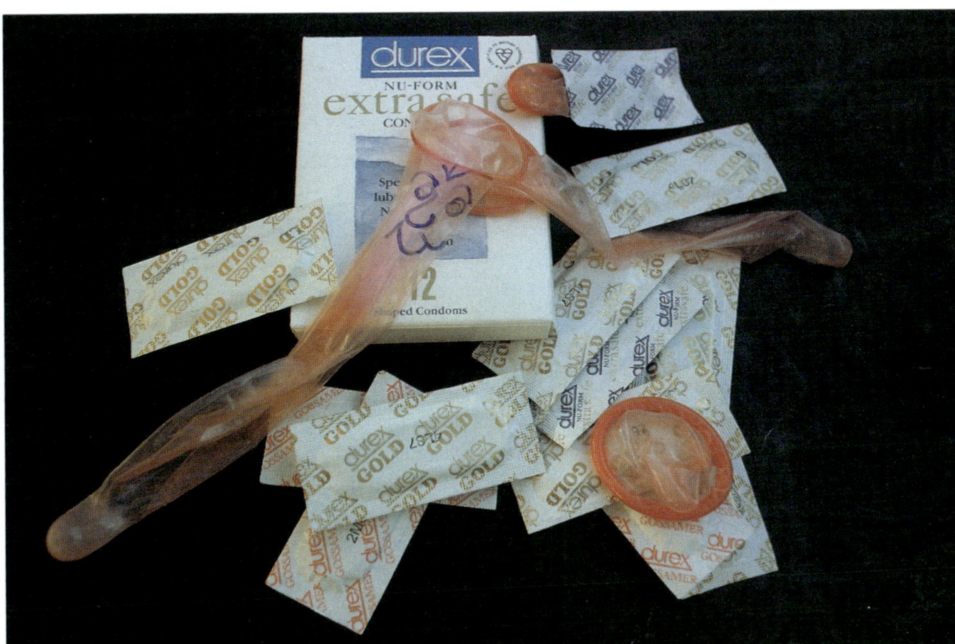

direct body contact that might spread HIV. Medical tests have proved that HIV *can't get through* a condom made of latex rubber. (So-called "natural" condoms made of sheep gut are not reliable because the virus may leak through them.)

Many prominent doctors, including Dr C. Everett Koop, the recent Surgeon General of the United States, believe that using condoms during sex *any* time you don't know if your partner might be HIV-infected is one of the best possible ways there is to prevent the spread of this disease. Using a sperm-killing foam or jelly along with the condom provides even more protection. The sperm-killing chemical **nonoxynol 9**, the main ingredient in most sperm-killing foams or jellies, kills HIV as well as sperm.

In order for condoms to protect you, you have to actually use them, and use them correctly. Here are some basic rules* for using a condom correctly for self protection:

(l) Use a condom *every single time* you have sex.
(2) The boy should put on the condom as soon as his penis is erect, before he has *any* contact with the girl's vulva or vagina.
(3) Roll the condom all the way down to the base of the penis before starting sex.
(4) Coat the condom with spermicidal jelly or foam before sex. This will make the outside slippery and keep the condom from tearing. *Don't* use vaseline or vegetable oil for this. These things make the rubber break down.
(5) The boy should pull his penis out soon after climax, before it gets soft, holding onto the rim of the condom so it doesn't slip off. That way there won't be any unprotected contact.
(6) Don't use the same condom more than once.
(7) To be extra safe, the girl should also put a spermicide into her vagina before sex. This provides extra protection against infection.

** Adapted from Hatcher, Robert, Contraceptive technology l986-l987, ed. 13. New York: Irvington Publishers, l987; and Goldsmith, Marsha F, "Medical News and Perspectives," Journal of the American Medical Association. May l, l987, Vol 257, No 17.*

Of course, if you work at it, you can find a lot of excuses not to use a condom. Some people say they're a nuisance and a bother. Some say they are "too embarrassed" to use them. Maybe your partner just doesn't happen to have one around at the right time. But if you are really interested in protecting yourself against HIV infection, you are the one who has to insist, whether you are a boy or a girl, and then stick to it. As one girl said, "When he told me he didn't have a condom, I just had to take a deep breath and tell him to go and get one."

Only time will tell how much these measures will, in the long run, really slow down the spread of HIV infection. But you don't have to wait to find out. Public health experts worry that many young people already understand the danger – and the ways to protect themselves – but just don't bother. That's sad for *them*. By "living defensively" you can protect yourself from ever getting this deadly infection – and that's what counts.

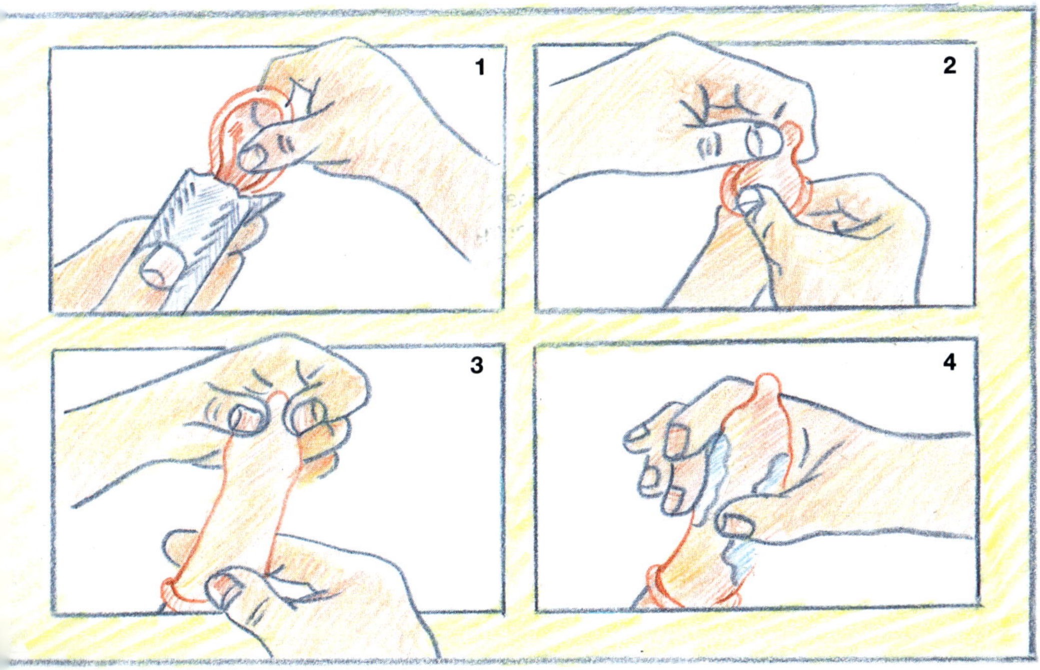

CONDOMS SAVE LIVES
ENCE=DEATH
CONDOMS for

Chapter Six:
Fighting AIDS

The campaign to promote safe sex is a vital part of the war against HIV, the virus which causes AIDS.

Ever since the very first cases of AIDS were seen in 1981, doctors have been asking two questions: *"What causes this disease?"* and *"How can we fight it and cure it?"*

The first question was easy to answer. Doctors soon learned that AIDS is the late end-result of infection by the Human Immunodeficiency Virus or HIV. They have since learned a great deal about that virus, how it behaves, and how the harm it does to the immune system can lead – in the long run – to the dreadful sickness we call AIDS.

But answers to the second question – how to fight this disease, or cure it – are coming very slowly. So far, nobody knows how to cure an HIV infection, or how to get rid of the virus once it invades a human being. Even when a person who seems perfectly healthy finds out that he or she has been infected, there is nothing much that doctors can do. The doctors have to wait and see if the virus begins to make that person sick and cause symptoms. In other words, no safe or useful way is known, at present, to fight HIV infection right from the start. Only when the *symptoms* of AIDS or AIDS-Related Complex begin to appear in an HIV-infected person can doctors start taking steps to fight the disease.

There are four possible ways doctors are trying to fight this infection:

(1) By finding drugs to attack the virus itself.

(2) By finding better ways to fight down the opportunistic infections or cancers that cause AIDS patients to die.

(3) By finding better tests to detect HIV infection early (so that it might someday be treated earlier).

(4) By finding a vaccine against HIV, so that people could be protected against infection in the first place.

Each of these matters offers promise for the future. Let's look more closely at each one.

Attacking the Virus

We know that antibiotic drugs can cure many deadly infections caused by bacteria. These drugs either kill the bad bacteria or prevent them from multiplying. Antibiotics today help cure strep throats, tuberculosis, gonorrhoea and syphilis, for example. But until recently, antibiotics just haven't worked at all against viruses. Now, as we learn more and more about *viruses*, this is changing.

(1) **Acyclovir.** A few years ago, for example, a drug called acyclovir (pronounced "ace-eye-clo-vir") was discovered. It could slow down the multiplying of a virus called Herpes Simplex Virus Type 2 or HSV-2. This is the virus that causes genital herpes, a sexually transmitted disease you've all heard about. Acyclovir doesn't *kill* that virus. It just cripples it, so it can't make new viruses very fast. But by doing this, the drug can reduce the number of outbreaks of genital herpes an infected person may have. It's not a cure, but it's a big help for people who have this unpleasant infection.

(2) **AZT**. So far, acyclovir seems to have little effect against HIV. But another drug called zidovudine, or **AZT**, does. AZT works inside the HIV-infected cell. It blocks the action of the enzyme chemical that HIV uses to produce new HIV particles. Again, this drug doesn't kill the virus, but it *does* seem to slow down the production of new virus particles in an infected person. As a result, many people with AIDS who have taken AZT have shown remarkable improvement. They have less severe opportunistic infections. In some patients with Kaposi's sarcoma, the cancer seems to get better or even clear up. In addition, this drug makes many AIDS patients feel better. This means that some can get out of bed and go back to their regular work again. Overall, tests have shown that AZT actually allows many very sick patients to live longer than they would without it.

Unfortunately, there are some difficult problems with AZT. It is extremely expensive. Many AIDS patients just can't pay for this drug without help. AZT is a very strong chemical that makes many people taking it develop anaemia (a very low red blood cell count) so they must have blood transfusions. About one third of all AIDS patients have such severe side effects from AZT that they can't take it at all. Because of these problems, AZT was first prescribed only for patients who were very sick with AIDS. But now some AIDS experts are giving the drug much earlier to some HIV-infected patients, hoping to postpone the late, deadly stages of the disease. Smaller doses are often effective, with fewer side effects.

As yet, nobody knows how helpful early AZT treatment may prove to be, or how long the good effects of the drug will last. But one final problem may limit its usefulness. Some patients using AZT seem to get less and less help from it as time goes on. The reason, scientists suspect, is that HIV, over time, learns to resist the effects of the drug, so that it does less and less good.

(3) **Other possible medicines.** Meanwhile, researchers are looking for

Counselling and medical advice help drug users overcome addiction.

other drugs that might work against HIV infection. One, known as CD-4, may be a future winner. Recently, scientists discovered one of the reasons that the HIV virus can attack T4-cells so easily once it gets into the body. The surface of the T4-cells were found to be covered with special protein molecules called CD-4. Those molecules were like doors into the cell. HIV particles had to hook onto these special molecules in the first place in order to get inside the T4-cells. Otherwise, HIV couldn't infect T4-cells.

Scientists have now found a way to manufacture special "look-alike" CD-4 molecules in huge numbers. They hope that these "phony" molecules, injected into a patient's blood, will trap and "tie up" new HIV particles before they can infect new T4-cells, and thus slow down the infection. Will this work? Nobody knows yet. It's just one possible new weapon against HIV infection.

Another experimental drug called DDI has recently been found to be almost as effective as AZT, in early tests, with far less serious side effects. More extensive tests are now under way. Still another possible weapon involves a chemical called GLQ223, found in the root of a Chinese cucumber plant. This chemical seems to kill infected T4-cells and macrophages – along with the viruses that are infecting them. Whether it will work against HIV, or be safe for humans, is not yet known.

Treating Opportunistic Infections

While scientists develop and test new anti-HIV drugs, they also look for better ways to treat the opportunistic infections that so often cause death in AIDS patients. *Pneumocystis carinii* pneumonia or PCP, for example, can often be held in check by a drug called TMP/SMX (short for trimethoprim/sulphamethoxizole). But this drug doesn't cure the infection, and many people have bad side effects from using it. Fortunately, another drug called pentamidine can also help with the pnuemonia infection. It is now widely used to treat or prevent PCP. Pentamidine seems to work best when the patient inhales a mist of it deep into the lungs.

Kaposi's sarcoma can often be treated with X-rays. But this doesn't *cure* the cancer, so other treatments are also being explored. For example, a natural body chemical called alpha interferon has been made in large amounts in the laboratory. This may help slow the advance of the cancer in some AIDS patients. But it is another "strong medicine" that can give the patient high fevers and other bad side effects. Overall, finding new ways to treat these deadly infections and cancers is one of the biggest challenges in the fight against AIDS.

Better Testing for HIV Infection

One thing is certain: as HIV infection spreads, it will be more and more important to find quick, inexpensive ways to detect it as early as possible. This is true for two reasons. First, the earlier an infection is spotted, the earlier the damage it may do can be slowed down by new treatments. Second, the earlier it is spotted, the better chance there is to prevent its spread, and keep our blood banks free of infected blood. At present many scientists are working to find better ways to test for HIV infection.

An HIV Vaccine

Of course, trying to treat HIV infection after a person is infected is an uphill fight. It would be far better to have a safe, effective vaccine to protect all of us against infection in the first place.

So far there isn't any such vaccine. Researchers are working hard to find one, but many problems stand in the way. First, we need something to use for a vaccine. This could be some part of the HIV that would cause the immune system to make anti-HIV antibodies without actually causing the infection. Then we would need to *test* the vaccine to be sure that it works,

Candles of remembrance are lit during an AIDS vigil.

and is safe to use. Such a vaccine would have to be tested in the laboratory and on animals before trying it on human beings. But the only animals other than humans that can be infected by HIV – and thus could be tested – are chimpanzees, and they are very scarce. Already several promising "candidate vaccines" have been made, but scientists fear it may take another five or ten years before we finally have a reliable HIV vaccine to use on humans worldwide.

Meanwhile, we have to do the best that we can with what we have. In this book we've seen what HIV infection is, and what AIDS is, in plain, simple terms. We've seen how people get infected. We've seen what kinds of treatment may help people who catch it, and above all, we have seen what you can do to protect yourself from ever getting it. You can't fight something you don't understand. But you can protect yourself from *this* infection, if you know the facts and use your common sense.

Glossary

Amoebic dysentery – an intestinal disease caused by a protozoan (an animal-like germ).

Antibiotics – drugs that kill germs in the body or keep them from growing.

Antibodies – special chemicals the body makes to travel in the blood stream and fight viruses and other foreign invaders.

Anti-HIV antibodies – antibodies the body makes to try to fight an HIV virus invasion.

ARC (AIDS-Related Complex) – an early group of AIDS symptoms, including diarrhoea, vomiting, weight loss or swollen glands, but without any signs yet of opportunistic infections.

Asymptomatic carriers – people infected with HIV who carry the virus and can pass it on, but do not yet have symptoms of AIDS.

AZT (zidovudine) – a drug which relieves symptoms and prolongs the lives of people with AIDS.

Bacteria – plantlike germs that cause many different kinds of infections.

B-cells – a group of lymphocytes (white blood cells) that help the body manufacture antibodies.

Candida – an infection, often in the mouth or throat, caused by a tiny yeast plant.

Enzyme – a special chemical in HIV which is needed for the virus to multiply.

Epidemic – an infection that spreads rapidly in the population.

Gonorrhoea – one of the most common sexually transmitted diseases or STDs, caused by a germ that attacks the urine tube or a girl's Fallopian tubes.

Genital herpes – an STD caused by a virus that produces outbreaks of painful sores on or around the sex organs.

Haemophilia – an inherited disease in which the blood doesn't clot properly.

Heterosexual – people who prefer having sex with members of the opposite sex.

HIV (Human Immunodeficiency Virus) – the name scientists today give to the virus that causes AIDS.

Homosexual – people who prefer having sex with members of the same sex.

Immune system – the body's natural defence system to fight off foreign invaders such as bacteria or viruses.

Immune system deficiency – any breakdown of the normal activity of the immune system. An HIV invasion can cause an immune system deficiency.

Infection – any invasion by bacteria or viruses which causes damage to the body.

Intravenous (IV) drugs – drugs which are taken by injecting them into a vein. Doctors often prescribe good IV medicines for very sick patients. But many drug users inject illegal drugs, such as heroin or cocaine, into their own veins with dirty needles.

Kaposi's sarcoma – a kind of cancer, usually very uncommon, which frequently occurs in people with AIDS.

Leukaemia – cancer involving the white blood cells and bone marrow.

Macrophages – special white blood cells that engulf and digest invading bacteria or viruses.

Micro-organisms – tiny living cells, such as bacteria, protozoa or viruses, too small to be seen without a microscope.

Nonoxynol 9 – a sperm-killing chemical that also kills HIV and can help prevent its spread during sex.

Opportunistic infections – infections that usually occur only when a person's immune defence system has broken down.

Parasites – organisms that live in other organisms' bodies, but give nothing in return.

Pathogens – germs that cause infections.

Plasma cells – white blood cells that manufacture antibodies.

Pneumocystis carinii pneumonia (PCP) – a kind of opportunistic lung infection common in people with AIDS, caused by a protozoan (animallike) germ.

Pneumonia – infection of the lungs.

Protozoans – single-celled animallike germs which can cause infections. Several opportunistic infections in people with AIDS are caused by protozoans.

Retroviruses – a special group of dangerous viruses which require the help of a special chemical or enzyme in order to multiply.

Rhinoviruses – viruses that enter the body through the nasal passages and cause infections such as head colds.

Semen – the fluid, containing sperm cells, that comes out of the boy's penis when he **ejaculates**, or comes, at the end of sex. HIV particles are often found in the semen of an HIV-infected person.

STD (sexually transmitted disease) – an infection passed from one person to another during sex.

Syndrome – a group of symptoms commonly occurring together in a disease or infection.

Syphilis – a dangerous and widespread STD.

T4-cells – a group of lymphocytes (white blood cells) that control and regulate the whole immune defence system.

Toxoplasmosis – an infection, often in the brain, caused by a protozoan.

Viruses – the tiniest of all disease-causing micro-organisms, visible only with an electron microscope.

WHERE YOU CAN GET HELP

Your family doctor may be able to help with general enquiries about HIV and your health. Also contact:

National AIDS Helpline
0800 567 123
Free phone from anywhere in the country (24 hours a day, 7 days a week).

Terrence Higgins Trust
52-54 Gray's Inn Road
London WC1X 8JU
071 831 0330
Helpline 071 242 1010
(3-10 pm every day)

Australia

Queensland AIDS Council,
Brisbane: 844 1990
Victorian AIDS Council,
Melbourne: 419 3166
AIDS Council of New South Wales,
Sydney: 211 0499
Northern Territory AIDS line,
Darwin: 411 711

Index

Photographic credits
Cover and pages 32 and 37: Franklin / Network Photographers; page 4: Lighthouse; pages 3, 9, 15. 17 and 22: Science Photo Library; pages 11, 39 and 42: Topham Picture Library; pages 12 and 25: Associated Press / Topham Picture Library; pages 20 and 29: Sturrock / Network Photographers; page 45: Sparham / Network Photographers; pages 52 and 59: Lowe / Network Photographers; page 56: Roger Vlitos.